BLACK HISTORY

Civil Rights and Equality

Dan Lyndon-Cohen

W

FRANKLIN WATTS
LONDON•SYDNEY

This edition 2020

First published in 2010 by Franklin Watts

Copyright © The Watts Publishing Group 2010

Editor: Tracey Kelly
Series editor: Adrian Cole
Art director: Jonathan Hair
Design: Stephen Prosser
Picture research: Diana Morris

Dan Lyndon-Cohen would like to thank the following people for their support in writing this book; The Black and Asian Studies Association (BASA), Marika Sherwood, Arthur Torrington, Joanna Cohen and Joanna Caroussis. Thanks also to the Lyndon, Robinson, Cohen and Childs families.

This series is dedicated to the memory of Kodjo Yenga.

Acknowledgements:

Alinari /Topfoto: 23b. AP/Topham: 27t, 35b. ©Jonathan Boast/City of Westminster Archives/Dover War Memorial Project: 16. W E B Du Bois Library,University of Massachusetts: 15b. Ken Brown/Shutterstock: endpapers. Cardiff Central Library: 19b. City of London/HIP/Topfoto: 5, 10b. Timothy A Clary/Getty Images: 8. CNN/Getty Images: 36bl. Mary Evans PL: 12cr, 25. Fotomas/Topfoto: 19t. FPG/Getty Images: 22tr. The Granger Collection/Topfoto: 13t, 28, 29bl, 29tr, 30t, 33t, 34, 35t. R L Hambley/Shutterstock: front cover r, back cover l. J B Helsby/Hulton Archive/Getty Images: 18. Hulton Archive/Getty Images: 13b, 17b, 21, 23t, 27b, 33b. Zoran Karapancev /Shutterstock: 6. Alisdair Macdonald /Rex Features: 9b. Museum of London: 10t. NPG London: 11t. PC/Peter Naum at the Leicester Galleries, London /Bridgeman Art Library: 15t. Photonews/Topfoto: 38, 39t. Photri /Topfoto: 37. Picturepoint/Topham: front cover l, back cover r, 24tr, 32, 36tr. Popperfoto/Getty Images: 22bl. Rollis Press/Popperfoto/Getty Images: 9t. Southwark Local History Library, Peckham: 20. Time Life Pictures/Getty Images: 30bl. Topfoto: 14, 24bl, 31b. UPPA/Topfoto: 39b. Jonathan Utz/Getty Images: 26. Watts Archive: 11b, 12bl.

Every attempt has been made to clear copyright.
Should there be any inadvertent omission please apply to the publisher for rectification.

PB ISBN: 978 1 4451 8080 9
eBook ISBN: 978 1 4451 8081 6

Printed in Dubai

Franklin Watts is a division of Hachette Children's Books, an Hachette UK company.

Carmelite House
50 Victoria Embankment
London, EC4Y 0DZ
www.hachette.co.uk

Contents

Introduction

Many people of African descent living in Britain and the USA today are linked by a common history: their ancestors were forced into slavery between the 16th and 19th centuries. Their struggle to achieve civil rights – the rights of all people to social and political freedom – has been hard fought.

Transatlantic Slave Trade

The Transatlantic Slave Trade resulted in millions of Africans being kidnapped and transported, against their will, to the Americas, the Caribbean and Europe by Europeans. From the 18th century onwards, there are many examples of people travelling between Britain and the USA to support the struggle against slavery and to improve the rights of black people.

▲ *Barack Obama and his family at his victory celebration. The Obamas are from African-American, English and Kenyan heritage.*

People such as the American activist W.E.B. Du Bois, who was one of the leaders of the Pan-African Movement, and campaigner Claudia Jones, from Trinidad, the 'mother of the Notting Hill Carnival', spent time fighting for better rights for black people in Britain. The campaigns of the Civil Rights Movement, with the inspiring leadership of Martin Luther King and the radical politics of Malcolm X, shaped events on both sides of the Atlantic.

Ending discrimination

Since the 1950s, there has been steady progress in civil rights, particularly in making discrimination in employment and education illegal, and in making opportunities for black people more widely available. In 2009, Barack Obama became the first US President to have African heritage. Some

▲ Over 100,000 people took part in this civil rights march in Washington, USA, in 1963.

people see this as a sign that race is becoming less of an issue in the USA.

However, the progress made in civil rights has never been smooth. The discrimination and racism that occurred in Britain and the USA in the 20th century has been challenged more effectively, but it still exists. Events such as the beating of Rodney King (see page 36) and the murder of Stephen Lawrence (see page 38) act as a stark reminder of how much further we still need to go to reach full equality for all citizens.

So what's inside?

Inside you will learn about the events and key people behind the fight for equality, from the abolition of slavery in the 1800s, to the election of the first mixed-race US President in 2009.

▲ The Pan-African flag, a symbol of black unity first used in the USA.

▲ The parents of Stephen Lawrence, who was murdered in London in 1999.

Nineteenth-century radicals

The slavery abolitionist movement united people. It inspired other protest movements, such as the Chartists who fought for the rights of all working people in Britain, and also led the way for civil rights and the active involvement of black people in politics. Two of the most important radicals of the 19th century were William Davidson and William Cuffay.

Cato Street conspirators

William Davidson was born c.1786 in Jamaica. His father was the island's Attorney General (lawyer) and his mother was a black woman. Davidson was sent to Scotland at the age of 14 to finish his education. Davidson became involved in radical politics after the Peterloo Massacre in 1819 (when the army attacked a political rights demonstration in Manchester). He joined a small group called the Cato Street conspirators, who plotted to assassinate members of the British

William Davidson (c.1786–1820)

▲ *This illustration shows the moment police went to arrest the Cato Street conspirators in 1820.*

government in 1820. However, a spy infiltrated the group, and they were all arrested and put on trial.

At the trial Davidson appealed to the court not to be prejudiced against him because of his colour. The judge replied, *"A man of colour is as much entitled to the protection of the law of England as the fairest man in the land. God forbid that, in the verdict of an English Jury, complexion should be taken into consideration."* Davidson was found guilty of treason along with four other men and was sentenced to death by hanging.

Did you know?

After Davidson and the Cato Street conspirators were hanged on 1 May 1820, their heads were cut off and displayed to the huge crowds. This was the last public decapitation (beheading) in English history.

The Chartist movement

The son of a former slave from St Kitts in the Caribbean, William Cuffay, who was born in Kent, became one of the first black men to become a leader of a political movement in Britain. Cuffay began his career as a tailor, and in 1834 joined a strike to improve working conditions. He then lost his job and became more active in the Chartist movement, which campaigned to get the vote for working men and improve the lives of working people.

In 1842, Cuffay became a leader of the London Chartists. Cuffay was one of the organisers of the massive Chartist demonstration in Kennington, London in 1848. Later that year he was arrested and found guilty of trying to start an armed uprising. Cuffay was sentenced to 21 years in prison and transported to Tasmania, Australia, where he died in 1870.

William Cuffay (1788–1870)

▲ *The Chartist demonstration in Kennington, London, in 1848.*

The Pan-African Conference 1900

The aim of the Pan-African Conference was to gather together Africans from the Caribbean, Americas and Europe to discuss the key issues that were affecting their lives. Their demands included equal civil rights for Africans, equal access to education and better opportunities for trade and business.

The African Association

In 1897, Sylvester Williams, a Trinidadian who had studied law in Canada and London, set up the African Association. Williams wanted to bring together African people from around the world and so set up the first Pan-African Conference in 1900, held in London. The phrase 'Pan-African' was used to describe the idea of Africans coming together to share their experiences and support each other in improving their lives.

▲ Samuel Coleridge Taylor (1875–1912) was a delegate at the Pan-African Conference in 1900.

There were 56 delegates at the conference including leading Americans such as W. E. B. Du Bois and Bishop Alexander Walters, who led the conference. There were also American women including Anna J. Cooper and Anna Jones. British delegates included John Archer (see pages 14–15), Samuel Coleridge Taylor, a composer, and the first British-Asian Member of Parliament, Dadabhai Naoroji.

▲ Henry Sylvester Williams (1869–1911) established the first Pan-African Conference.

Civil rights issues

During the three-day conference delegates debated important topics. The titles of presentations included 'The Trials and Tribulations of the Coloured Race in America' (by Bishop Walters), 'The Negro Problem in America' (by Anna J. Cooper) and 'The Preservation of Racial Equality' (by Anna Jones). They also discussed the legacy of slavery, the impact of Christianity on Africa, African history before European involvement, and how to support the independent black states of Haiti, Sierra Leone and Ethiopia.

Letter to the world

At the end of the conference, W. E. B. Du Bois led a committee to decide how to implement the ideas that had been discussed. They wrote a letter entitled 'Address to the Nations of the World', which said: "The problem of the 20th century is the problem of the colour line." It was sent to leaders of countries around the world.

▲ Anna J. Cooper (1858–1964) wrote one of the papers debated in 1900.

Press report

The Pan-African Conference of 1900 was reported in the *Picture Post* (right) and in newspapers, including the *Westminster Gazette* which quoted Sylvester Williams: *"I felt it was time some effort was made to have us recognised as a people, and so enable us to take our position in the world... Our object now is to secure throughout the world the same facilities and privileges for the black man as the white man enjoys."*

John Archer

In the decades following the abolition of slavery, progress was slowly being made for the civil rights of Africans living in Britain. When black people began to enter politics, the issues that Africans faced were better recognised and their rights better represented. The first black mayor in English history was Dr Allan Minns, Mayor of Thetford in Norfolk, in 1904. Then, in 1913, John Archer became the first black person born in Britain to be elected as mayor.

▲ John Archer (1863–1932) was the first British black mayor who had been born in Britain.

Rise to power

John Archer was born in Liverpool in 1863. His father was born in Barbados and his mother was Irish. Archer travelled overseas, where he met his Canadian wife, then moved to London and set up a photographers' shop in Battersea around 1898. He became involved in politics and was elected as a local councillor for the Progressive Party (Liberal) in 1906, serving on the council for the next 20 years. On 10 November 1913, Archer was elected Mayor of Battersea by 40 votes to 39. The *Daily Express* newspaper reported the news the following day:

"For the first time, it is believed, in the history of local government, a man of colour was yesterday elected Mayor of an English borough."

Historic speech

The *Daily Express* also quoted a speech made by John Archer to the people of Battersea:

"My election tonight marks a new era. You have made history…That will go forth to all the coloured nations of the world. They will look to Battersea and say: 'It is the greatest thing that you have done. You have shown that you have no racial prejudice, but recognise a man for what you think he has done.'"

John Archer had been one of the participants in the 1900 Pan-African Conference, and was an important supporter of the Pan-African cause. He also attended the 1919 and 1921 Pan-African congresses, chairing a session at the 1921 Congress, and was president of the African

▲ *A sketch of Battersea from the River Thames. John Archer became mayor of Battersea in 1913.*

Progress Union from 1918–1921. After many years in local government fighting for equality and civil rights, he died in 1932 at the age of 69.

▲ *Delegates at the 1921 Pan-African Congress held in Belgium. John Archer is third from right.*

World War I

World War I (1914–18) was a truly global conflict, with fighting taking place not only in Europe but also in Africa. The British Army included soldiers from every corner of the British Empire. There were 15,000 men in the British West Indies Regiment and over 50,000 Africans in combat units. In 1917, the USA joined the war. Of the 367,000 African-Americans in service, just 40,000 were in combat roles.

Banding together

The impact of World War I on race relations was significant in many ways. Soldiers felt that the prejudice they experienced in their daily lives was not replicated in the trenches. George Blackman, a soldier in the British West Indies Regiment (BWIR), commented: *"When the battle starts, it didn't make a difference. We were all the same. When you're there, you don't care about anything. Every man there is under the rifle."*

First black officer

Walter Tull was a mixed-race Englishman who played professional football for Tottenham and Northampton Town. In 1914, he joined the Footballer's Battalion of the Middlesex Regiment. After fighting at the Battle of the Somme in France,

▼ *Dover War Memorial Project commemorating the life of Walter Tull.*

Tull was invited to attend the Officers Training School in Scotland. He completed the course and became the first black officer in the British Army to take command of white soldiers. This was highly significant because prior to Tull, there had only been black officers in the medical corps – Tull had broken the army's colour bar (ban on black people having the same rights as white people). Just before his death in action in March 1918, Tull was recommended for the Military Cross.

The Taranto Mutiny

After the war ended in November 1918, the British West Indies Regiment was transferred to the British military base at Taranto, Italy. Here they would be demobilised (the process that soldiers go through before returning to civilian life). However, due to a shortage of labour, the BWIR

soldiers were told that they had to build toilets for white soldiers. They also discovered that white soldiers were being given a pay rise and black soldiers were not.

As a result, many soldiers refused to follow their orders and the 'Taranto Mutiny' began. Black officers were beaten up and one was killed. The following day, 60 BWIR sergeants met and formed the Caribbean League. Their mission statement was that "the black man should have freedom and govern himself in the West Indies and that force must be used, and if necessary, bloodshed to attain that object". The British Army acted swiftly and the ringleaders were rounded up and punished with long prison sentences. The BWIR was quickly disbanded once troops had returned to the Caribbean and there were no welcome parades to celebrate their contribution to the war effort.

Did you know?

Many African and Caribbean soldiers, like these, were recognised for their bravery in World War I, with 300 being awarded medals. The war also politicised many black soldiers who were prepared to fight for better rights for black people.

▶ These African-American soldiers are returning from World War I. They are wearing the Croix de Guerre (Cross of War) of France which they received for bravery,

Race riots

At the end of World War I, hundreds of thousands of men returned home. Black British and African soldiers went home to cities such as Liverpool, Cardiff and London. Unfortunately, these industrial and port areas were hit by a dramatic increase in unemployment and tension began to build, particularly over competition for jobs. Black people's rights were ignored, and violence erupted in the form of race riots in Liverpool, which then spread across the British Isles.

Liverpool riots

As a former port for slave ships, Liverpool had been home to black people for hundreds of years. By 1919, the black population had risen to 5,000 and post-war competition for jobs was tough. Some black workers were sacked, even though

▲ *An African-American troop band marches through London at the end of World War I.*

they had been working since before the war. Shortly afterwards, attacks on black people started to take place on the streets of Liverpool. One attack led to retaliation from the black community, but the response from the police was a massive raid on their homes. A young black man called Charles Wotten was chased down the road near the docks by a huge mob. He was thrown into the water and drowned, yet no arrests were made.

Over the next few days, thousands of rioters swarmed the streets attacking any black person they could find, smashing windows and destroying houses. One potential solution that was offered was to pay for some black people to be returned to Africa or the Caribbean. However, when a ship offered 200 places, only 40 were taken up. Most of the black community in Liverpool saw themselves as British and wanted to stay in their homes. They would not be chased away by racists.

▼ *Riots like this took place in Liverpool in the early 20th century as a result of social tension and unemployment.*

▼ *A photograph of Butetown, Cardiff c. 1900.*

Conflict in Cardiff

There was even worse tension in Cardiff. In June 1919, a black man was accused of making an offensive remark to a white woman. A fight broke out and crowds began attacking the homes of local black people. A mob of 2,000 people went rampaging through the streets of Cardiff, attacking not only black properties but also Chinese laundries.

Eventually, the situation came to a head and the black community decided to defend itself with weapons. Community leaders talked to the police and it was agreed that 600 black men would return to live in the Caribbean, but the rest would stay and should be protected by the law.

The League of Coloured Peoples

In the 1920s and 1930s, the racial tension that erupted after World War I eased slightly. However, there was still a huge amount of prejudice and discrimination against black people in Britain and the USA. The most obvious sign of this was the colour bar, which made it very difficult for black people to find good jobs and housing, and to feel accepted in society.

Professional ban

The medical profession was particularly difficult for black people to get into, with one black woman being refused work at 25 hospitals on the 'grounds of colour'. The evidence from her case was recorded in *The Keys*, a journal run by the League of Coloured Peoples – set up by Dr Harold Moody in 1931. *The Keys* also featured articles, reports and poetry that showed the frustration black people felt as a result of their poor treatment in Britain.

League of Coloured Peoples

Harold Moody was born in Jamaica in 1882 and travelled to England to study medicine at Kings College, London in 1904.

▲ *A view of a Peckham street in the 1930s, where Dr Moody established himself.*

Not only did he find it incredibly hard to find decent housing, but after qualifying as a doctor with excellent results, he was denied a hospital position because the matron 'refused to have a coloured doctor working at the hospital'. After other hospitals also rejected him, Dr Moody set up his own practice in Peckham, London, which became very successful. He started to campaign for improvements in the lives of black Britons and in 1931, set up the League of Coloured Peoples.

The first meeting of the League established four main aims, followed by a fifth in 1937:

1. To protect the social, educational, economic and political interests of its members

2. To interest members in the welfare of coloured peoples in all parts of the world

3. To improve relations between the races

4. To co-operate and join with organisations sympathetic to coloured people

5. To give financial assistance to coloured people in distress as lies within our capacity.

Improved rights

The League of Coloured Peoples campaigned for better rights by writing to the media and MPs, and by holding public meetings. One famous success came about when it got the BBC to apologise after a broadcaster used the word 'nigger' (a powerful, racist word referring to black people) on air. The League also arranged social events and activities, particularly for young black people. These included camping and boat trips. This was important as many urban, young, poor people would not have otherwise been able to experience life outside the city.

▲ Dr Harold Moody (1882–1947) set up the League of Coloured Peoples in 1931.

Extract from Disillusionment, a poem by Sylvia Lowe

"Here we have learnt the difference, here we see
That we are barred by colour in this land
To which we gave so great a loyalty …

We go a disillusioned British host
Back to the lands from which we came of late
Forever broken by our welcome here
And all the bitter insults we meet."

The Keys, vol. 1, 1933

World War II

As in World War I, the outbreak of World War II (1939–45) saw men and women from Africa and the Caribbean join black Britons and Americans in the armed forces. Around 372,500 African troops fought in Burma and East Africa. Troops from the Caribbean were mostly volunteers, including 5,800 in the Royal Air Force. Some joined because they wanted to fight against fascism, which supported racist ideas. Some hoped that the contribution black people made would be repaid with more independence for countries in Africa and the Caribbean.

▲ A Jamaican RAF gunner in the cockpit of a bomber during World War II.

War effort

From 1941, the British government began to actively recruit men and women from the Caribbean to join the war effort. Over 12,000 men joined the Royal Air Force and about 600 women joined the Auxiliary Territorial Service, working as drivers, carpenters and electricians. Posters were sent out to Africa and the Caribbean encouraging workers to contribute. Raw materials such as palm oil, rubber and tin were shipped to Britain in huge quantities. There is even evidence of African countries collecting extra taxes to contribute to the war, with over £1 million being given to the British government from the West African colonies.

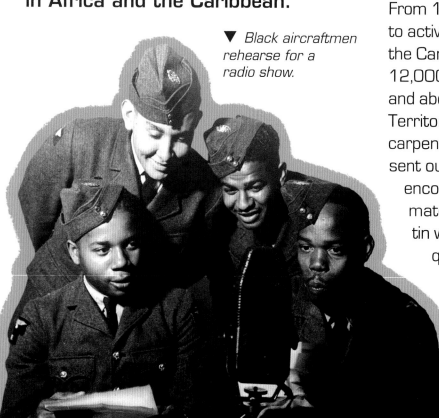

▼ Black aircraftmen rehearse for a radio show.

◀ Black women from the Auxiliary Territorial Service arrive at camp in 1943.

The home front

The League of Coloured Peoples (see pages 20–21) recorded the contributions that many black people made on the home front during World War II. These ranged from joining air-raid patrols to working with the fire brigade. Black entertainers such as jazz singer, Adelaide Hall, and bandleader, Ken 'Snake Hips' Johnson, performed during the war.

▲ Adelaide Hall (1901–93) was born in Brooklyn, USA and performed throughout World War II.

The Americans arrive

After the USA entered the war in December 1941, thousands of soldiers came to Britain to fight in Europe. Over 10,000 were African Americans and their arrival created some tension. The US Army was effectively segregated, with black and white soldiers being kept in separate units (this was not the case in the British Army, although there were separate West Indies regiments). The racist attitudes that were held in America were also apparent in Britain, and there was particular concern about black soldiers having relationships with white women. Many fights broke out and the government even had to make recommendations that, at least in the armed forces, black and white people should avoid each other.

However, after the war, the rights of black service people slowly improved. In 1947, the British Cabinet decreed that the armed forces should continue to accept volunteers from the UK's ethnic minority community.

Windrush generation

In the years that followed World War II, new black immigrants arrived in Britain from the Caribbean on ships such as the *Empire Windrush* and others. This led to the creation of new black communities – and new racial tensions. However, these vibrant communities paved the way for the rich multi-cultural society that Britain has become today.

Lord Kitchener

The song 'London is the Place for Me' – see opposite – was written by Aldwyn Roberts (also known as Lord Kitchener), a Calypso singer and songwriter from Trinidad. Kitchener emigrated to England in 1948 on board the *Empire Windrush*.

▲ *Some of the people on board the* Windrush. *Many of the immigrants were young men.*

His lyrics show the optimism that the new influx of black immigrants arriving in Britain after World War II felt about living in the 'Mother Country'.

Sadly, this did not last, as the issues that had dominated the lives of black Britons for many years still continued. The colour bar was still in existence and this meant poor living and housing conditions and difficulties in finding well-paid jobs.

▲ *The* Empire Windrush *brought people from the Caribbean to start a new life in the UK.*

Shipping in

The *Empire Windrush* docked in Tilbury, Essex on 21 June 1948, carrying 492 Caribbeans from Jamaica and Trinidad. Many of them had served in the armed forces and some were hoping to find jobs again, particularly in the Royal Air Force. Others were seeking work in the newly created National Health Service or for London Transport. Because many of the men on board the *Empire Windrush* did not have a place to stay, over 200 were taken to the deep shelter at Clapham Common in south-west London. This was underneath the tube station and had been used to hold prisoners of war during World War II. However, within a month, nearly all of the immigrants had found jobs. Many stayed in the area and formed new communities in places like Brixton, Peckham and Camberwell.

The legacy

The people of the 'Windrush generation' established communities that for the first time meant there were large numbers of black people living in different parts of Britain. By the early 1960s, there were an estimated 125,000 people of Caribbean descent living in Britain (along with 55,000 Indians and Pakistanis). Many of the new migrants were highly skilled but worked in jobs that were far below their qualifications. They had to face discrimination and prejudice sometimes on a daily basis. Yet these women and men were able to build thriving communities and make a positive contribution to post-war Britain, paving the way for the diverse, multi-ethnic population that exists today.

▲ *A group of men on Southam Street, London, in 1956. Most men had not planned to stay in Britain for more than five years.*

"London is the place for me
London, this lovely city ...

To live in London you are really comfortable
Because the English people are very much sociable
They take you here and they take you there
They make you feel like a millionaire."

**London is the Place for Me,
Lord Kitchener, 1951**

Claudia Jones is known as the 'Mother of the Notting Hill Carnival', an annual festival that has been running for 50 years and is now the biggest street party in the world. However, her story is about much more than the Carnival – Claudia Jones was also a very important campaigner for black rights in the USA and Britain.

▲ *Young carnival dancers capture the bright spirit that Claudia Jones injected with her work.*

Early years

Claudia Jones was born in Trinidad in 1915 and moved to Harlem, New York in 1923. Harlem was then a very deprived area, with poor housing and limited opportunities for the black community living there. Jones was community-minded even as a child – at her junior high school, she won the Theodore Roosevelt Award for Good Citizenship. However, in 1932, she contracted tuberculosis, a lung disease which cut short her education and affected her health throughout her life.

Journalist and communist

In the 1940s, Jones became a journalist and also joined the American Communist Party. In 1948, she became one of the editors of the *Daily Worker*, the Communist Party newspaper. Jones travelled around the USA giving speeches and campaigning for improvements to the lives of working people. However, at that time, there was a lot of anger and mistrust directed against communists. Many were accused of being 'un-American', particularly by Joseph McCarthy, a member of the US Senate. Jones was arrested four times and eventually deported from the USA to Britain in 1955.

The *West Indian Gazette*

Claudia Jones arrived in London at a time when there was an increase in racial tension. In the summer of 1958, there were race riots in Nottingham and Notting Hill, west London. In May 1959,

▲ *Police clash with protestors during the Notting Hill race riots in August 1958.*

a young black man named Kelso Cochrane was murdered by six white men, who were never put on trial (the case is similar to that of Stephen Lawrence in 1993 – see pages 38–39). Jones established the *West Indian Gazette* as a newspaper that would campaign for better rights for black Britons, as well as highlight contributions being made by black writers, artists and performers.

The Notting Hill Carnival

In January 1959, in response to the Notting Hill race riots, Claudia Jones helped launch the first indoor Notting Hill Carnival in St Pancras, London, which celebrated Caribbean culture, dance and music. The Carnival kept growing until 1965, when it was so big it had to be held outdoors. Sadly, Claudia Jones died on Christmas Eve, 1964 aged 49, brought on by a heart condition caused by tuberculosis.

▲ *The funeral procession of Kelso Cochrane. No one was ever charged with his murder.*

Roots of the Civil Rights Movement

There are many parallels between the struggle for equality and civil rights for people of African heritage in Britain and in the USA, from the 16th century to today. The most obvious reason for this is the connection between the two countries that occurred as a result of the Transatlantic Slave Trade.

Emancipation Proclamation

In 1830, there were over two million enslaved Africans (or their descendents) in the USA, with the vast majority living in the South. The slaves worked on huge plantations growing crops such as tobacco, cotton and sugar, and the conditions were terrible. In 1861, a civil war broke out between people in the

▲ *Members of the US Colored Infantry in 1865, who took part in the American Civil War.*

Southern states who wanted slavery to continue, and people in the North who wanted slavery to be abolished. In 1862, President Abraham Lincoln declared the Emancipation Proclamation, which said that slaves would be set free in the Southern states. The American Civil War ended in

1865 with victory for Lincoln and the abolitionists. The 13th Amendment of the Constitution was passed and slavery ended throughout the USA.

Reconstruction

The ending of slavery did not mean that the lives of African Americans improved immediately. The government tried to help freed slaves by setting up organisations such as the Freedman's Bureau, which aimed to help them find jobs and obtain medical treatment. Most importantly, the Bureau funded 1,000 schools so that the huge problem of illiteracy (not being able to read and write) among the African-American population could be tackled.

However, there was still a lot of prejudice and discrimination as a result of white racist attitudes. The Jim Crow 'separate but equal' Laws ensured there was segregation between blacks and whites. For example, on buses there were seats assigned for the white passengers at the front and for black passengers at the back. Schools were segregated too.

◄ Even drinks machines were segregated by law.

▲ Members of the NAACP protest against segregation laws in Texas, USA, in 1947.

The NAACP

One of the most terrifying racist crimes against African Americans was lynching (hanging). A large gang would attack someone who was accused of a crime and punish them, often by lynching. Many African Americans were killed this way. Organisations such as the National Association for the Advancement of Colored People (NAACP) were formed to stop lynchings. The NAACP also campaigned to improve the rights of African Americans. W. E. B. Du Bois, a founder-member (see pages 12–13), set up *The Crisis* newspaper to publish material dedicated to the cause. By 1919, there were over 90,000 members of the NAACP, with centres in over 300 US cities.

Martin Luther King and civil rights

The campaign for civil rights for African Americans really took off in the 1950s. By this stage, the NAACP focused on providing a legal challenge to the discrimination that still existed in the USA, particularly in the areas of education and voting rights.

Supreme Court success

In 1954, the first major success for the NAACP was the winning of a case at the Supreme Court, known as Brown versus The Board of Education of Topeka, Kansas. The NAACP was able to prove that segregated education was very harmful to black children and was unconstitutional (against the rights of US citizens). The Supreme Court agreed and segregation in education was ended.

▲ Rosa Parks (right) sits on a bus in 1956. Earlier that year buses had still been segregated.

The Montgomery Bus Boycott

In December 1955, Rosa Parks, a member of the NAACP in Montgomery, Alabama, was on the bus home when she was arrested for sitting in a seat reserved for white passengers. As a result, thousands of black Americans decided

◄ African American women walk during the bus boycott in 1956.

not to use the buses in protest. This became known as the Montgomery Bus Boycott and the main organiser was a man called Martin Luther King Jr, who was the president of the Montgomery Improvement Association.

King believed in a policy of 'passive resistance', which meant that he urged his supporters not to use violence under any circumstance. The bus boycott was so successful that it lasted for 381 days and the bus companies lost 80% of their income. Finally, in November 1956, the buses in Montgomery were desegregated.

The Civil Rights Movement

Inspired by ideas of Martin Luther King and successes in desegregation, new civil rights organisations formed. The Student Nonviolent Coordinating Committee (SNCC) called for sit-ins across the USA to make restaurants and public places allow blacks and whites to sit together. Another campaign was about voter registration. African Americans had been given the right to vote after slavery was abolished. However, many were too frightened to use their votes after being threatened by white racists or by having to take difficult literacy tests. The NAACP, SNCC and CORE (Congress Of Racial Equality) all joined together to register as many African Americans as they could.

For many African Americans, changes in their lives came about very slowly. Some people argued that the civil rights campaign was not effective enough. King realised that one of the most important ways of improving people's lives was by improving their living conditions and pay. He turned his attention to the fight against poverty but was tragically assassinated on 4 April 1968.

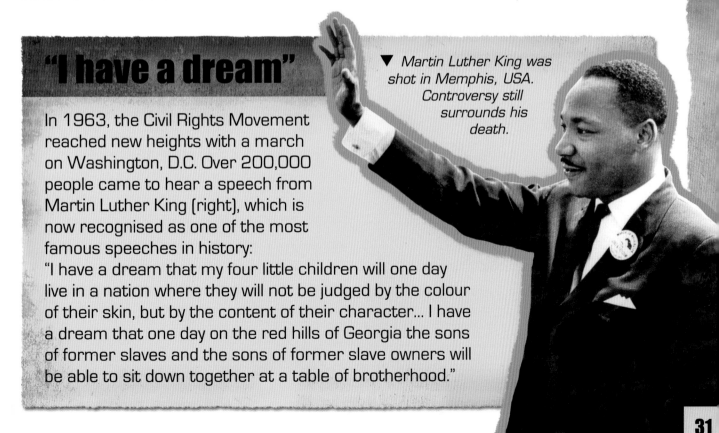

"I have a dream"

In 1963, the Civil Rights Movement reached new heights with a march on Washington, D.C. Over 200,000 people came to hear a speech from Martin Luther King (right), which is now recognised as one of the most famous speeches in history:
"I have a dream that my four little children will one day live in a nation where they will not be judged by the colour of their skin, but by the content of their character... I have a dream that one day on the red hills of Georgia the sons of former slaves and the sons of former slave owners will be able to sit down together at a table of brotherhood."

▼ Martin Luther King was shot in Memphis, USA. Controversy still surrounds his death.

The civil rights laws

The growing support for the Civil Rights Movement in the early 1960s meant that pressure was increasing on the US president to introduce further legislation (laws). Some civil rights laws had been introduced by President Eisenhower in 1957 and 1960, but their impact was limited. When John F. Kennedy became president in 1960, he promised more changes. However, his assassination in 1963 meant that two important acts were introduced by his successor, Lyndon Johnson.

The Civil Rights Act 1964

A Civil Rights Commission reported in 1960 that the standard of living for African Americans was significantly lower than that of white people. Life expectancy was seven years lower, the infant mortality rate (number of babies dying before their first birthday) was double the rate of white babies and over 50% of housing was considered unacceptable. Kennedy realised that something needed to be done, but his death meant that Lyndon Johnson took responsibility for passing a new Civil Rights Act.

The US Congress passed the law in 1964 after a lot of opposition, particularly from the Southern states, where there was still segregation. The law made segregation in public places illegal and created an Equal Employment Commission to make sure that African Americans were not discriminated against in the workplace. It also made sure that money was not provided to employers or schools that were still segregated. Although this law was an important step in the right direction, many African Americans were disappointed that it did not go further. They were still concerned about their voting rights and so the campaign turned to this issue.

▲ *John F. Kennedy takes the presidential oath to become the 35th US President in 1961.*

▲ *President Johnson signs the Civil Rights Act.*

The Voting Rights Act 1965

There was a violent response to the 1964 Civil Rights Act, particularly in the South, with African Americans protesting at the lack of progress and white racists attempting to prevent black people from registering to vote. President Johnson introduced the Voting Rights Act in 1965, and it passed through Congress. The law stated that the only requirement to vote was American citizenship, so the literacy tests and financial requirements that had been used to prevent African Americans from voting were now illegal. There was a massive increase in the number of African Americans registering to vote and wanting to run for political positions.

▲ *Police confront a group of people protesting about the Civil Rights Act in Alabama, USA, 1965.*

The rise of Black Power

Despite the success of Martin Luther King and the NAACP in persuading the US government to pass laws, such as the Civil Rights Act (see page 32), some African Americans believed that progress was too slow. They turned to more extreme leaders and organisations, such as Malcolm X and the Black Panther Party.

Malcolm X

Malcolm Little was born in Omaha, Nebraska in 1925. His father, Earl, was a Baptist minister and a civil rights campaigner, who was murdered by white racists in 1931. As a young man, Malcolm moved to Harlem and became involved in petty crime, eventually serving 10 years in prison for burglary. While Malcolm was in prison, he began to follow the teachings of a black Muslim called Elijah Muhammad (1897–1975), and converted to Islam.

Nation of Islam

Muhammad was the leader of the Nation of Islam, an organisation that believed African Americans needed to take control of their own destiny; building their own communities for economic, political and social success (called separatism). After leaving prison in 1952, Malcolm became a leader of the Nation of Islam and changed his surname

▲ Malcom X (1925–65) gives an interview to press reporters in Washington, 1963.

to 'X' to show he rejected his 'slave name'. He delivered radical speeches, calling white people 'devils', and attracted media attention. He rejected King's ideas of non-violence.

However, Malcolm X left the Nation of Islam in 1964 to focus on the idea of black power – the belief that African Americans should be more positive about themselves and their goals. He also accepted that blacks and whites needed to work together to tackle racism. On 21 February 1965, Malcolm X was assassinated – three Nation of Islam members were convicted of his murder.

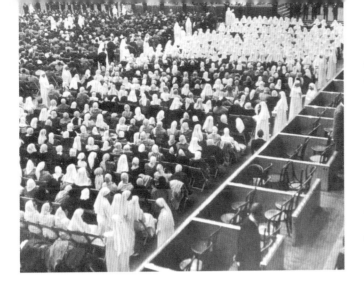

▲ *Elijah Muhammad addresses a meeting of the Black Muslims in Chicago, c. 1960.*

The Black Panther Party

Another group that was disillusioned with the lack of progress in the Civil Rights Movement was the Black Panther Party (BPP), formed by Huey Newton and Bobby Seale in 1966. The BPP wanted to improve the lives of African Americans and was prepared to use more violent methods to achieve it. Their manifesto (set of beliefs) focused on education, housing, healthcare, employment and civil rights. They wanted black history to be taught in schools, free healthcare, co-operative housing projects and protection from police brutality.

There were often confrontations between the BPP and the police. The BPP was seen as a significant threat to the US government and, as a result, the FBI effectively destroyed the movement. By the mid-1970s, the BPP began to focus more on providing support for African-American communities and became much less involved in using violent protest.

▼ *Members of the Black Panther Party wearing their military-style clothing in 1969.*

Race in the USA today

The path towards greater equality in the USA has not always been smooth. The great strides forward that have been made in recent years, including the election of Barack Obama, have also been matched by continuing tension.

Los Angeles riots

In March 1991, an African-American man named Rodney King was driving home in Los Angeles, California when he was caught speeding by the police. After a car chase at over 185 kph, King was finally stopped. But when he stepped out of the car, he was badly beaten by four police officers. The whole episode was caught on film and, as a result, it was brought to the attention of the media. Many Americans were outraged at the brutality shown. It raised questions about the treatment of

▼ Rioters torched cars and buildings after the Rodney King trial.

African Americans by the police, as well as drawing attention to their continued low status in American society.

The subsequent trial found the police not guilty of assault, and this led to rioting in Los Angeles in April 1992, when outraged people swarmed the streets and caused over US $1 billion of damage. In the end, 53 people were killed, over 7,000 fires were started and the police, National Guard and US Army were called in to stop the riots.

MAR. 3 1991

▲ Los Angeles police are captured on film beating Rodney King in the street.

Nearly 30 years after the Civil Rights Movement, it was clear that there was still work to be done to make African Americans truly equal. The chance of an African-American male ending up in prison was still higher than his chance of attending a university. African Americans still had a lower life expectancy than whites and were less able to afford healthcare insurance. Unemployment was higher and educational achievement was lower than white Americans.

First African-American president

Yet this is only part of the story. There have been large steps forward since the civil rights campaigns of the 1960s. The standard of living for all Americans has risen significantly and African Americans now occupy senior positions in business, law and education, as well as in sports and music. The swearing-in of Barack Obama in January 2009 made history, as he became

▲ *Barack Obama takes the presidential oath to become the 44th US President in 2009.*

the first man of African heritage to become a US president. Many people saw this as a sign that racism and discrimination would now come to an end. However, as Obama acknowledged in a speech in July 2009:

"We've got to say to our children, yes, if you're African American, the odds of growing up amid crime and gangs are higher. Yes, if you live in a poor neighbourhood, you will face challenges that somebody in a wealthy suburb does not have to face. But that's not a reason to get bad grades, that's not a reason to cut class, that's not a reason to give up on your education and drop out of school. No one has written your destiny for you. Your destiny is in your hands — you cannot forget that."

Race relations in the UK

The first UK law to tackle discrimination on the grounds of race was the Race Relations Act, passed in 1965. However, this was ineffective, and needed to be improved. The Race Relations Act of 1976 made it illegal to discriminate against anyone on the basis of race in employment and education. Under the Act, an organisation called the Commission for Racial Equality (CRE) was set up to monitor discrimination.

Stephen Lawrence

Although there was some progress in tackling racism in Britain after the 1976 Race Relations Act, occasional events have challenged the advances that have been made. The death of a young black Briton, Stephen Lawrence, in 1993 was a watershed moment in many ways. Stephen was walking home in London on the evening of 22 April when he was murdered by a gang of five white men, alleged to have called him racist names. The subsequent failure to find enough evidence to convict the five men of the crime led to an investigation into the Metropolitan Police Force's handling of the case. The Macpherson Report of 1999 called the police "institutionally racist" (a term coined by Black Panther Party leader, Stokely Carmichael). As a result, 70 recommendations were suggested, including making it illegal to make racist comments even in private. Training on race equality issues in police forces was called for, as well as in schools, the National Health Service and other large organisations.

▼ *Teenager Stephen Lawrence, who was murdered in Eltham, London in 1993.*

Did you know?

In the UK, key individuals such as Dr Harold Moody (see pages 20–21) and Claudia Jones (see pages 26–27) inspired organisations such as CARD (Campaign Against Racial Discrimination) to fight for better treatment for black Britons.

▲ *Flowers surround the memorial to Stephen Lawrence on Walworth Road, London.*

The Equality Commission

In 2006, the Equalities Law was passed and a new organisation called the Equality and Human Rights Commission (EHRC) was set up, headed by a black Briton named Trevor Phillips. The Commission's role was "to eliminate discrimination, reduce inequality, protect human rights and to build good relations, ensuring that everyone has a fair chance to participate in society". Although it has come under some criticism for its lack of progress, the Commission is still recognised as having an important role to play in the fight for civil rights and equality.

The struggle for equal rights in the United States and the United Kingdom has a long, painful history and still has a long way to go. However, it is a struggle that has ultimately made both societies more just and better places to live for all people regardless of their heritage. The fight continues, and in the words of Martin Luther King: "We will not be satisfied until justice rolls down like waters, and righteousness like a mighty stream."

▲ *Trevor Phillips was head of the CRE and then its successor, the EHRC.*

Timeline – Civil Rights and Equality

1807 Abolition of the slave trade

1820 Cato Street Conspiracy – execution of William Davidson

1833 Abolition of slavery in parts of the British Empire

1848 William Cuffay (the black Chartist) arrested and exiled to Tasmania

1862 Emancipation Proclamation declared by President Lincoln to free slaves in Southern US states

1865 13th Amendment to US Constitution abolishes slavery in the USA

1900 First Pan-African Conference takes place in London

1904 Dr Allan Minns becomes the first black mayor in Britain for Thetford, Norfolk

1909 NAACP formed to fight for civil rights for African Americans

1913 John Archer becomes the first black Mayor born in Britain, when he is elected as Mayor of Battersea, London

1914 World War I starts, with soldiers from Africa, Asia and the Caribbean fighting alongside soldiers from Britain

1916 Walter Tull becomes the first black officer in the British Army to take command of white soldiers

1919 Race riots in Cardiff, Liverpool, London, Glasgow and South Shields

1931 Dr Harold Moody forms the League of Coloured Peoples

1939 World War II, starts with soldiers from Africa, Asia and the Caribbean fighting alongside soldiers from Britain

1948 *Empire Windrush* arrives with 492 immigrants from the West Indies

1954 Brown v.Topeka court case ends segregation in education in the USA

1955 Rosa Parks arrested for sitting in the white section of a bus in Montgomery, Alabama

1958 Race riots in Nottingham and Notting Hill

1959 Notting Hill Carnival established

1963 The march on Washington, D.C. Martin Luther King's 'I have a dream' speech

1964 Civil Rights Act passed in the USA

1965 Voting Rights Act passed in the USA, Malcolm X assassinated, first Race Relations Act passed in the UK

1966 The Black Panther Party formed by Bobby Seale and Huey Newton

1968 Martin Luther King assassinated

1976 Race Relations Act in the UK sets up the Commission for Racial Equality

1991 Rodney King beaten by L.A. police officers

1993 Murder of Stephen Lawrence

1999 Macpherson Inquiry establishes that the Metropolitan Police were guilty of 'institutional racism'

2009 Barack Obama becomes the first mixed-race President of the United States

American events

British events

Websites and Bibliography

Websites

http://www.blackpast.org/?q=perspective
s/pan-african-congresses-1900-1945
Detailed overview of the Pan-African conferences.

http://www.hartford-
hwp.com/archives/30/057.html Interesting
article on the contribution of women
to the Pan-African movement.

http://www.movinghere.org.uk/galleries/
histories/caribbean/settling/keys.htm#
From the Moving Here website, an excellent
microsite about the League of Coloured Peoples.

http://www.bbc.co.uk/history/british/
modern/arrival_01.shtml
Interviews with *Windrush* pioneers.

http://www.malcolmx.com/
An interesting website that includes a biography and
quotations.

http://www.thekingcenter.org/
DrMLKingJr/
The official Martin Luther King website, which has
lots of images and details about his life and work.

Bibliography

Adi H, *The History of the African and
Caribbean Communities in Britain,*
Wayland, 2007

Dabydeen D, Gilmore J and Jones C (Eds),
*The Oxford Companion to Black British
History*, OUP, 2007

File N and Power C, *Black Settlers in
Britain 1555–1958*, Heinemann, 1995

Fitzgerald S, *On the Front Line,
Struggling for Civil Rights*, Raintree,
2005

Fryer P, *Staying Power, the History of
Black People in Britain*, Pluto Press,
1984

Hoyles M, *The Axe Laid to the Root, the
story of Robert Wedderburn*, Hansib
Publications, 2004

Osbourne A and Torrington A, *We
Served, The Untold Story of the West
Indian Contribution to World War II*,
Krik Krak Publishing, 2005

Torrington A, *Windrush Pioneers*,
Windrush Foundation, 2008

Glossary

Abolitionist
Someone who wanted to abolish the slavery of Black Africans.

Americas
The word used to describe all the lands of both North and South America.

Attorney General
The chief legal officer of a place.

Boycott
Refuse to have anything to do with a product, a country or a means of transport.

British Empire
The United Kingdom and all the lands under its power. It reached its largest extent after World War I.

Cabinet
The most important ministers of a government.

Chartist
A member of a political group that worked for changes to the political system in Britain in the 1830s and 1840s.

Civil rights
The rights of all people to social and political freedom.

Colony
An area or country controlled by another country.

Colour bar/Colour line
Preventing black people from doing certain jobs or activities with white people.

Constitution
The main principles used to govern a country.

Discrimination
Unfair treatment of a person or group because of their race, sex or beliefs.

Emancipation
Freeing someone from the control of someone else.

Home front
The activities of the population of a country at war.

Immigrant
Someone who moves to another country to settle.

Infiltrate
To carefully and secretly join a group, in order to spy on them.

Life expectancy
The usual number of years that someone is expected to live.

Matron
A senior nurse in a hospital.

Media
The name for newspapers, radio, the Internet and TV.

Mixed race
The child of parents of different races, for instance a white British man and a black African woman.

Nation of Islam
An organisation founded in 1931 by black American Muslims.

Pan-African
Of, or for, all Africans, including those who live in countries other than those on the African continent.

Plantation
Large farms that enslaved Africans were forced to work on, growing crops such as sugar, tobacco and cotton.

Prejudice
An opinion or dislike formed against something or someone.

Race riot
A riot caused by hatred for people of other races living in the same community.

Radical
A person who has bold new ideas and actions – and wants extreme social or political change.

Segregation
Separation or isolation of a race of people from the rest of the community. In the USA this led to separate schools, restaurants and housing districts for black and white Americans.

Slavery
When someone is forced to work for another person and loses all of their freedom and rights.

Sovereign
A supreme ruler. In the UK, the sovereign is the king or queen.

Transatlantic Slave Trade
The name given to the enslavement and forced removal of millions of Africans from Africa to the Americas between the 16th and 19th centuries.

Transportation
To send criminals abroad to a foreign country as a punishment. Once there, they had to work for a set amount of time, or even for the rest of their lives, on projects such as road building.

West Indies
Large group of islands in the Caribbean Sea and including Barbados, Jamaica, Antigua and the Turks Islands.

Index

These are the lists of contents for the titles in *Black History*: